About the author

Tom Binns has worked in the entertainment industry for several years – as both a success and a failure. He is one of the presenters on the Channel 4 early-morning programme RI:SE and before that he presented Tom Binns' Breakfast on 104.9 XFM. He's worked with the great and the good of show business, including Steve Coogan, Davina McCall, Jamie Oliver and Angus Deayton. This is his first book.

D1227319

How To Get Famous

How To Get Famous

Tom Binns

First published 2002 by
Prion Books Limited
Imperial Works, Perren Street
London NW5 3ED
www.prionbooks.com

Text copyright © 2002 Tom Binns

ISBN 1-85375-501-X

A catalogue record of this book can be obtained
from the British Library

Cover design by Grade Design Consultants
Printed and bound in Great Britain
by Creative Print & Design Ltd, South Wales

Contents

Introduction

Fame is wonderful. It's easy money and it's an easy lay. Everyone wants to know you and be your friend. Once you're famous you can earn thousands of pounds just by telling people which shampoo you use or that you like certain cakes. You won't have to queue up to get into night-clubs, and if you get the fame game right you'll have newspaper hacks and photographers hounding you morning, noon and night for the latest showbiz exclusive.

With a little effort getting famous is easy and, with the punters' insatiable appetite for reality game shows, fly-on-the-wall documentaries and soap operas, you don't even have to have any special ability or talent to make it big.

If you don't fear shame and have an instinct for self-promotion you too can climb the celebrity ladder. And all the entertainment magazines and TV channels with a slot to fill will help you thrust yourself into the punters' faces, until they love you almost as much as you love yourself.

But fame isn't just for those who love themselves. The adoration of a nation and the constant attention of the tabloids is the perfect antidote to low self-esteem, especially when you can mask the emptiness inside with illegal drugs, showbiz parties and plenty of alcohol.

Many people think they will be no one until everyone knows who they are. In reality, if you are an unknown loser, becoming famous is just a way of letting the rest of the world know how sad you are. But that's OK – there's real comfort to be had fromknowing the world is taking an interest in your personal life, and the nation's press will work hand in hand with your PR agent to make sure the punters' appetite for you will be satisfied. You'll be able to bare your soul and share your darkest secrets and the punters will lap it up. (Even secrets you might think were better kept private.) You'll feel so much better once you see them splashed all over the front pages of the Sunday papers.

After all, a problem shared is a problem halved. Imagine how much easier coping with a personal tragedy will be when you have the whole world discussing every detail of your pain. You can't buy therapy like that.

But remember, fame isn't just about you and your problems. When you become famous you become the property of the people who put you there: the members of the public. They have given you the power of fame and they can just as easily take it away from you. Or so you make them think. In reality, they don't lift a finger to help you. They just sit at home on the sofa stuffing their faces with the cake you r ecommended, occasionally popping out to the shops to buy a copy of *Hello* or your latest CD, and deep down they feel bad about their sad, little lives and envy your exciting one. So it's important to tell them that your fame is all down to them. This stops them feeling so bad, and means they won't stop buying your CDs.

If you are ready and determined to grab your own piece of fame and you don't mind putting in some effort then I can help you. We'll work out exactly what you have to do in order to achieve fame, and to cash in on it once you've made it. I'll also offer you some useful advice on how to stay famous, and if you ignore that then I can offer you a few tips to cope with life as a has-been.

Ninety-eight per cent of the fame business is illusion and lies. The other two per cent is bullshit. The key to guaranteeing fame is spotting the lies, separating them from the illusion and bullshit and then using all three to your advantage. It's easy when you know how. Think of this book as the dog Toto from *The Wizard of Oz*. He pulled aside the curtain of illusion to reveal the wizard for who he really was. If you've got the stomach for it, I'm ready to tear asunder the glitzy curtain that hides the grim truth about fame. Are you ready to be Dorothy? Then let's skip up the yellow brick road to fame.

Definitions

A Punter is anyone who isn't famous, but believes all the hype surrounding fame. A punter reads celebrity magazines, enjoys daytime television and buys the barbecue sauce with the picture of their favourite TV Chef on the label, even though the other barbecue sauces on the shelf have the same ingredients and cost less. A punter will follow a star around the country, go to every concert, buy all the videos and CDs and wait for hours in the rain for an autograph.

Punters fund the multimillion-pound fame business. They are under the illusion that they can make or break stars. They are made to feel very much in charge when they buy the merchandise or vote for their favourite band, but in reality they have little or no say in the fame business. Punters are constantly used, manipulated and conned by the experts running the show who ensure the maximum amount of cash can be milked out of them at all times.

A Famous Punter is a famous person who believes his own hype. Famous punters usually have someone behind them pulling all the strings and taking a large cut of their earnings. Famous punters can be mainly found in the music industry. They are usually young kids in bands earning a few quid doing what they enjoy and making millions for their managers.

Most people aren't famous and don't believe or don't care about the hype. They wouldn't make a special journey to the book store to get a book signed by the latest TV DIY expert. However, if they were already in the book store or passing in the street they might look over to see what all the fuss was about. At a push they'd buy the book and get it signed. Not for themselves, of course. For their mum, who's 'a big fan'. After all, we've all got a little bit of the punter in us ... haven't we?

Naked ambition

Before we go on any further let's just remove any doubt you may have in your mind about your ability to get famous. Here are a few things to consider:

★ You're not going to make it unless you really believe in yourself. You really need to think you're it.

★ Do you love yourself enough to be famous? It really helps if you love yourself in a way that many people would consider unnatural.

★ Try thinking about how much you love yourself now. If you find this embarrassing and awkward it might help if you start to touch yourself in a loving way. If you're reading this book in public you might prefer to go home first before you really start to show yourself how much you love you.

★ When you think about it, you're not setting yourself unrealistic targets in your ambition to become famous, are you? You only have to be better than the worst famous person there is. How hard can that be?

★ Just watch TV for five minutes. Sooner or later someone rubbish will come on the screen. Do you see? You only have to be better than them.

★ A lot of people think that fame is all in the hands of the gods and that famous people are born, not made. If you are one of those people then you need to empty your head of that nonsense right now. Think like this and you'll fail. Just look at some of the losers who are famous. Do you think any god worth his salt would pick them?

★ However, belief on its own is not enough – you also need inside knowledge. You need to know what fame is before you can achieve it.

Here's the dictionary definition:

famous adj.
Well or widely known

As you can see from this, fame boils down to a very simple principle. It is just a question of making sure that other people know who you are. That's more or less all there is to it. Once you've got a reason to be famous (don't worry, these days this can be quite flimsy) then it all boils down to marketing.

Fame is just something you create in the minds of the people around you. The punters' perception is that you must be good at what you do because you are famous, but really all you need to be good at is getting famous.

Other skills will be helpful, as you will learn later, but you don't have to be the world's best cook to be a world-famous cook. You simply need to be a cook who's well-known.

That's all there is to fame. Simply put, the more people who know you, the more famous you will be. You don't need to become a special person, you don't need to change in any way.

To illustrate the point, why don't you try the following exercise using direct mail? Direct mail is the most cost-effective method for selling products but so far it has been never used by anyone who wants to get famous. If you used this method to get famous not only would you be breaking new ground but I'm sure you would find the results, in terms of building up a fan base, very exciting.

Write a letter that is brief and to the point. Why don't you copy out my example on the next page? Don't forget to insert your name instead of mine, otherwise your campaign will backfire and I'll end up famous instead of you.

To Whom It May Concern:

My name is Tom and I'm a [insert your skill here]. You probably don't know me, but hopefully you do now.

All the best, Tom Binns

It might be a good idea to enclose a photograph and a stamped addressed envelope for the recipient to reply. Maybe you could suggest they return the photograph in the stamped addressed envelope. That way you could re-use it and save some money on printing costs.

However, it's not enough for people just to know who you are and what you do. When you read publicity about famous people you'll notice that it normally gives you insights into their personal lives. It is important to give the punters something they can hook into, so that they think they are bonding with you on a personal level. Information about a personal tragedy is great for this. Maybe you could adjust the letter accordingly:

> *To Whom It May Concern:*
>
> *My name is Tom and I'm a [insert skill here]. You probably don't know me, but my favourite kind of fish is sea bass and I was bullied as a child.*
>
> *All the best, Tom Binns*

Once the punters feel they know you and have shared your pain then it's time to flog themsomething:

To Whom It May Concern:

My name is Tom and I'm a [insert skill here]. You probably don't know me, but my favourite kind of fish is sea bass and I was bullied as a child. Why not buy my book, How To Get Famous? *It's available from all good bookshops.*
All the best Tom Binns

It's important here that you choose your own favourite kind of fish and don't just copy mine. Also, if you weren't bullied as a child, leave that bit out of the letter and replace it with another personal tragedy – preferably one that you've managed to overcome. Punters love the idea of the underdog overcoming all the odds – it gives them hope. It's important to be creative and original. As it happens, I wasn't bullied as a child. I just used that to illustrate a point. I do happen to like sea bass though.

If you really want to make sure your campaign works you could follow up your mailshot with a cold call on the telephone. You'll find the most productive time to call is in the early evenings. Why not read from this script:

> *Hello, I'm [Insert your name here], the [insert skill here]. I'm just ringing because I sent you a letter and photo of myself the other day and I wondered if you had any questions?*

At this point you should wait for the questions and field them accordingly. If you get stumped by a difficult question hang up and move on to the next number.

Note: Don't forget to block Caller ID before you make your calls. Check with your phone service provider for details.

You could try and supplement your

campaign by putting up posters in the areas where you send your letters. Some of the more adventurous of you might try dropping in on a couple of the people you spoke to on the phone. Who knows, a concerned resident might tip off the press about your campaign, and they might do a feature on you.

This may seem like a silly way to get famous, but it's a method that has worked for the most famous and powerful men in the world. At the heart of any US presidential campaign there are teams of people cold-calling and sending out mail-shots. The campaign is backed up with posters, door knocking, TV advertising and magazine interviews.

This is the only way anyone gets famous. Stars may prefer to use television, radio, newspapers or glossy magazines instead of direct mail to introduce themselves to the punters. But at the end of the day, when they give interviews on the television and in magazines all they are saying is, 'Hi, I'm this guy/this is what I'm like/here's a little piece of my personal life/now that we've bonded please buy my stuff.' It all boils down to the same thing.

This is the essence of getting famous. If you follow this procedure you will get famous too and if you use direct selling for long enough I can guarantee you will be as big as your phone bill.

Note: It is important that once you are famous you keep the true nature of fame to yourself. Once everyone realises how simple getting famous is, they'll all want a crack at it and this will make staying famous a whole lot harder than it is. Fortunately, most people involved in the fame business play to the rules and kid on that the whole industry is much more mystical than it really is.

Once you get famous the question you will

be most often asked by show business journalists is, 'What is it like to be famous?' Unimaginative entertainment editors love to hear the answer to this question. It's an opportunity to keep the fame myth going so trot out some such nonsense as:

'Being famous is like being a member of an exclusive club.'

'It's really the strangest thing to be recognised by people you've never met.'

'I feel very humble and special to be chosen for such an honour.'

What you mustn't say is:

'My publicist and I have made a real effort to get a lot of people to know who I am and so I can hardly be surprised that a lot of people now know who I am.'

For your own sanity it is vital that as you become famous you always remember this simple truth:

THE ONLY THING THAT CHANGES WHEN YOU BECOME FAMOUS IS OTHER PEOPLE'S OPINIONS OF YOU.

Unless, of course, you want to let the whole fame thing go to your head, in which case by all means lose all sense of proportion and turn into an arrogant, insecure, unstable tosser. It seems to work for a lot of people.

So how many people need to know who you are before you can say you are famous? Well, there are no official figures published on this matter, which is a great shame as it means the whole system is open to abuse.

A case in point is a supermarket in Staveley, a little town in north-east Derbyshire. They have a small cafeteria serving teas, coffee and snacks including a meal they describe as their 'World-Famous All-Day Breakfast', which consists of two eggs, one sausage, two pieces of bacon, a fried slice, a choice of beans or tomatoes and tea or coffee. I was suspicious of their claim and decided to do some research into the matter:

★ I called the British Consulate General in Jerusalem to ask if the local community there had heard of such a breakfast. They hadn't.

★ According to my sources at the Consulate General in Ekaterinburg, no one in the Russian Federation had heard of this breakfast either. Some Russians, I was informed, understood the concept of a full English breakfast from Western magazines and films but nothing specific about a breakfast from Staveley, Derbyshire.

★ Further enquiries showed that no one had heard of the meal in Tibet, Iceland or Nicaragua.

★ What was even more astonishing was that not even the people going about their business in Staveley had heard of the breakfast, although one or two people knew the supermarket 'did food'.

★ I even had to point out the meal on the menu to the waitress so that she 'could get an order number for the chef'.

Clearly, this breakfast isn't famous and neither is the extra large piece of cod and large portion of chips you get on the seafront in Brighton, described as 'Harry's World-Famous Fish Supper'.

I'd estimate that to get world-famous you need a large proportion of the planet to know who you are *and* what you do. Let's say about forty per cent to be safe. Just knowing who you are is not really enough. There's no point going through the long, humiliating and harrowing process of getting famous simply to be stopped by every passerby saying, 'Oh, you're that bloke, aren't you? You know, the one off that advert or was it a sports show? Where do I know you from, mate?'

Being stopped in the street by people who actually make a point of not recognising you is slightly worse than being ignored all together.

Note: It is tempting to think you can become famous simply by adding the words 'the world-famous...' before your name, as with the fish supper or the all-day breakfast. This used to work but people aren't as stupid as they once were, although you may still get away with it on the Working Men's Club circuit. One exception to this rule is if you're a singer who's recently been on a cruise or on a foreign holiday. This can entitle you to the prefix 'Internationally World-Famous'.

There are no real shortcuts to the big time. You'll have to be hard-working and determined and you'll need to know how to play the game. There are a few lucky exceptions to the rule and by all means use these as an excuse to justify not putting in any effort yourself – if you want to fail. But as the industry catchphrase goes, 'Fame costs and this is where you start paying'.

You might not like the idea of hard work. In fact, many people want to get famous because they think that it means having an easy life. This is not so. If you are one of these people and you've kept the receipt for this book why not see if you can get a refund? Tell the shop assistant that it was an unwanted present or something.

If you are prepared to go the distance you will have to work hard to get your big break and put in the effort to be ready when it finally comes.

It's all very well hanging around the theatre on the off chance the leading lady will break her leg tripping over a sandbag a careless stagehand has left lying around, but if you haven't learned her lines and you can't act then you're wasting your time.

Note: If you do manage to land a job as a stage hand don't even think about leaving a sandbag lying around! Get someone else to do it, and if they get caught deny all knowledge of them *and* the sandbag.

Be realistic, don't dream. You hear a lot of talk about dreams coming true in the magical world of show business; this is just the crap that gets trotted out to make the theatre more interesting and to drag in the punters. Which of these stories interests you the most:

'Fantastic new musical premiering on Friday night!'

or...

'Regular guy just like you plucked from obscurity doing a crap job just like yours stars in a fantastic new musical premiering on Friday night.'

If you want a piece of the action you have to get real. Do you have a realistic picture of who you are? If you're a 45-year-old bearded man with a pot belly you need to take a long, hard look at yourself and decide whether or not you have missed your window of opportunity to be the leading dancer with the Royal Ballet. It doesn't matter how many hours you wait outside the stage door in that stained mac waiting to look at the 'ballerina ladies'. It's not going to happen for you. Don't worry though, all is not lost – there is a route to fame for everyone. Why don't you consider being an archaeologist expert or a weather man for the BBC?

Punters are always being misled as to

the true nature of show business. Those running the fame business will do anything to put their stars up on pedestals well away from the mere mortals. In fact, the only difference between you and a celebrity is special lighting, quality film stock, clever staging, maybe a wig, designer clothes, make-up and a bit of air-brushing, plus a PR team that is expert at creating stories for the press. You'll need confidence to carry it off, but that comes with knowledge and practice or a couple of lines of coke.

Here are a few of the common myths about the fame game that build a psychological barrier between the famous and their punters. These myths are very useful because they keep the punters in their place and stop them getting ideas above their station and having a crack at fame themselves.

It's not what you know, it's who you know.

(Well, for a start, grammatically it's whom you know.) The reality is that the opportunity to become famous requires *both* what you know and who/ whom you know. There's no point being best mates with the President of MGM if when it comes to acting you're a complete vegetable. (Unless you are built like a Greek god and hung like a donkey.)

This classic myth has been around for ages. On the surface it sounds true and anyone can quote it down the pub and sound like an expert. It also works as a comfort blanket for the lazy, as it enables them to stay in the pub on their fat arses rather than do the necessary work needed in order to be a success.

The famous love this phrase because as long as punters believe it they'll stay in the pub and won't develop the talents needed to threaten their cushy position. It's a win-win situation – everyone's happy.

It's all about being in the right place at the right time.

This is another phrase invented to make punters think that fame is all down to luck, to stop them from making an effort and getting a life. If it's as simple as being in the right place at the right time then surely all one has to do is go to the right place and wait for it to be the right time. Oh, and don't forget: while you're waiting, learn the skills so that when the right time comes you'll be ready. Later in this book we'll cover all the right places you'll need to wait for the right time.

I just need a lucky break.

Have you learned nothing from the above? I feel like I'm banging my head against a wall. Hard work always beats luck. One of those success gurus from the States said, 'Luck is when opportunity meets preparation' and he's absolutely right. I can't remember his name but he had a tan and bleached teeth and you can buy his tapes in motorway service stations, I think it might have been Dale something...

To summarise, this is the only maxim you will ever need about fame:

If you spend enough time understanding how the fame game really works and then train your mind to cut through all the illusions and lies that show business generates, and if you persevere at developing all the necessary skills and contacts that are essential for success, then eventually you will be famous, as long as you don't piss too many people off along the way.

It's not very pretty or comforting is it? I don't think it'll catch on. Most people won't like it because it puts all the responsibility on them for success.

If you're not serious about getting famous and you're just a casual reader hoping to pick up some words of wisdom so that you can sound clever next time you're down the pub, then you should try this maxim instead:

You've either got it or you haven't. If you quote this it'll sound like you know what you're talking about and it'll help you rationalise never making any effort or taking any risks. It should also make you feel a lot better about being a loser and never really making it with that band you had. I think it's your round next.

Why do people want to get famous?

In the old days, when no one really travelled outside his or her town or village, everyone was famous – or to use our dictionary definition, everyone was well or widely known and everyone knew what everyone else did. The butcher, the baker, even the village idiot was famous and had a function. Everyone felt special.

These days we don't have that village atmosphere. Most of us work in anonymous jobs where we're herded together like cattle into call centres to be voices on the end of a phone; voices that haven't really got a clue why your computer keeps crashing or what the number is for the Crucible Theatre box office. I think this is one reason why so many of us want to be famous – this and the fact we've been taken in by the photographs in the celebrity magazines, so most of us think the life of the famous consists mainly of posing outside a country house in borrowed designer clothes with a perfect husband and beautiful new baby. What the magazine didn't photograph was the row the couple had that morning when the baby puked all down the designer dress.

Life Before Fame

The first steps to knowing what it is you want and how you're going to get it

By now you should be in no doubt of your own ability to make it. Remember, every time you are unsure just switch on your TV and take a look at some of the muppets that have made it. This will give your confidence a real boost.

I hope you now understand that anyone can get famous as long as:

★ Their attitude is right.

★ They have the right kind of inside information.

★ They learn the necessary skills.

★ They put in the necessary effort.

★ They don't piss off too many people.

It's now time to take some action. Let's focus on you. Get a piece of paper and write down how famous you want to be. I know this sounds like one of those sad exercises middle managers are forced to do when they have been sent away to run around some forest to find their inner selves but writing it down is the best way to get it clear in your mind.

These are the questions you will need to answer:

> What do you want to be
> widely known for?

This will be the core skill that will get you famous in the first place.

> Where do you want to be
> famous or widely known?

Do you want to be a local celebrity or an international superstar? This may have a bearing on what core skill you choose. There are very few internationally known DIY experts. You may need to concentrate on acting or singing, for example.

> How will you measure your fame?

What needs to happen before you realise you've made it? Will it be your picture in the paper or getting recognised in the street? Or will you only be satisfied once you get assassinated? You need to be clear about this from the start so that you'll know when you've arrived.

What you want to do when you're famous and why you want to be famous?

Take a careful look at your answers to these questions. If your goals can be achieved any other way than being famous you might save yourself an awful lot of wasted time and unnecessary hassle. If you like the look of being famous from what you've seen on the telly or in magazines, then by the end of the book you may have had some of your delusions shattered. You might change your mind about getting famous and decide to do something boring instead, like caring for the sick.

Just thinking about these questions won't be enough. You have to write down the answers to get a clear perspective on them. In fact, that's not enough either. You have to be specific and detailed in your answers. The more detailed you are in your answers, the more effective this exercise will be and the greater your chances of getting famous.

Tragically, many wannabes don't have even vague answers to these questions. 'I just wannabe famous' isn't good enough. There are millions of wannabes out there who have some vague notion of one day becoming famous. They don't know what they'd like to be famous for, they don't know how famous they want to be ... they don't really know exactly what being famous is. They've bought the glossy magazines and think it's going to be something like that but in 3D. It's not really fair to call them wannabes – they're *neverbes*.

Once you get clear on this subject and work out exactly what you want, you are already way ahead of the pack.

The skill or skills you need to make you famous are usually only an entry point to fame. They open the door, but once you are inside the world of fame you will find that it is a self-perpetuating cycle. Once you are famous you can dispense with the original skill that got you there and just focus on being famous for being famous. This involves eating at the right places, being photographed for magazines, being seen going to the right parties/film premieres and appearing on celebrity panel games. Here is a list of skills that could help to get you famous:

★ Any sport

★ Cooking

★ Writing (books or journalism)

★ Acting

★ Local radio presenting

★ Stand-up comedy

★ Some DIY

★ Modelling

★ Gardening

★ Music or singing

★ Astrology

★ TV Criticism

It is best to stick to something off this list. You may think to yourself, 'If we can have celebrity carpenters and decorators, why can't we have celebrity spot-welders?' My advice to you would be not to waste your time breaking new ground in this area. If you are a handy spot-welder try and get famous using one of the above skills – then you can use your fame to get people interested in your spot-welding abilities. True, our magazines and televisions aren't filled with articles and programmes about spot-welders and you may have found a gap in the market. But on the other hand, consider the remote possibility that there simply isn't the demand. Punters may not yet be ready to worship a spot-welder. When they are, the potential for merchandising is going to be huge. One lucky celebrity is going to get his name plastered all over acetylene torches and goggles in every DIY store in the land.

Once you've chosen the skills that you're going to use you can then identify where the kind of places you can go and practise or work with those talents. These are the places referred to in the phrase 'the right place at the right time'. Once you have your assets you can go to the right place and wait. For example, if you've decided that your core skill is going to be telling jokes then obviously the right place for that is a comedy club. You see, unlike making sure a navigational satellite stays in a geo-stationary orbit, getting famous isn't rocket science.

Fortunately the days are gone when

abilities were honed over years of hard work in rep theatre or music halls. These days learning a core skill is a lot easier. Memorise a few recipes and *voila*, you're a TV chef. If you're not very good at cooking you could get away with it by specialising in food for single mums or students. If you don't like cooking, read a book on the stars, develop a vague writing style and – hey presto – you're an astrologer.

What's interesting about skills is that the more you have, the longer you're likely to be famous for. Conversely, the more specialised you are the shorter your lifespan. Remember that bloke who used to do impressions of birds? No, neither do I. If you can present television, sing, dance, work with MDF, write books and act in films then you'll never be off our screens – although you will drive people mad, as no one likes a smart arse.

To get famous you don't have to be the best there is in your chosen field, although this is usually the punters' perception. You simply have to look as if you know what you're doing. The best doctors in the world aren't sitting on pastel couches in a TV studio telling old ladies to wrap up warm for the winter because a cold snap is on the way. Oddly enough, they're in hospitals saving lives.

On TV style and appearance are always more important than content and reality. If you want to be a **TV doctor** don't worry about having to remember anything from medical school because on TV everything is faked and before you even begin your slot you will be briefed on all the questions that you will get asked and you'll get plenty of time to research the answers.

It works the same way for most TV professions. **TV chefs** have people doing all the cooking and washing up for them off camera. The 'one they made earlier' was usually made by one of their assistants.

TV soccer pundits usually have an anorak sports fan who furnishes them with all the vital statistics before their half-time analysis. Ex-player soccer pundits were usually far too busy playing the game than to memorise all the names of the goal scorers from the past 20 years, so they need to rely on someone much sadder than themselves for that kind of information.

If you want to get famous by the **media pundit** route the only thing that matters is not what you know but how you deliver what you know. It is better to know nothing but appear to know what you are talking about than actually to be an expert in your field but appear not to have a clue. This is tragic. This is television.

My advice to you now is, no matter what core skill you choose, buy a video camera and practise talking to it. Make it your friend. You're not going to get famous unless you look good on television. This is the daddy of all the core skills and it is important that you get it right. If you look good on screen you can get away with murder.

What TV producers are looking for and what punters like is someone who looks and sounds relaxed. You have to look at the camera and speak to it as though it's your best friend. If you can do this you'll be way ahead of all the thousands of scared, wooden and stressed-out celebrities who are already making a good living from presenting television badly.

Study carefully the good people on TV and see what differentiates them from the bad. Listen to their tone and intonation. Would they speak like that if they were talking to their best friend in a pub? Often the answer to this question is 'only if they were mental'.

The only way to get relaxed in front of a camera is to practise and then watch the tape. If you get all squeamish about seeing yourself on TV or hearing the sound of your own voice, grow up and get used to it. Remember, if you do this right you're going to be on TV all the time. If there's something you don't like about the way you speak or look change it. Practice makes perfect.

Here are some of the core skills that you can choose to get you famous. Where possible I've mentioned the right places in which to wait for the right time to come.

Radio Presenter

One route into the world of media is radio. If you ask a radio presenter, 'Which do you prefer – presenting radio or presenting TV?' the answer they always give is, 'Presenting radio.' Until the day they are offered a job on TV.

Getting into local radio can be tough, but there are more openings than there used to be for someone who is cheap and willing to learn. The smaller stations aren't even bothered about whether you are willing to learn. You just have to be cheap – well, actually, free.

The key to getting on is to practise at home or in an empty studio whenever you can so that you can make a good demo.

It's always very difficult to get any respect at the first station where you learn the ropes. No matter how long you stay there you'll always be the boy or the girl who answers the phones and makes the tea. So when you feel that you've learned all there is to know and you've put together a strong demo tape then get the hell out and move on.

The best way to get a job at a radio station is to bombard them with emails and letters. Offer to answer phones or be a technical operator. Just hang on in there and try and make friends with the DJs.

TV Runner

A lot of stars started off as runners. Once you are a runner you can make your way into production and from there into TV presenting.

The key to being a good runner is networking (there's a section on that later in the book), doing what you're told and doing it well. If you want to make the next step up into production you must learn by keeping your eyes peeled and asking questions.

And remember the golden rule of show business: never admit you want to get famous. Hide your ambition, otherwise you'll be out of the door in seconds.

Being a TV runner is a great job as it puts you in the right place ready for the right time, which makes it a great job for networking. The only drawback is that you can be in the right place for 18 hours a day, often on little more than the minimum wage while you wonder if the right time will ever come.

Model

Market research is now revealing that consumers feel threatened by good-looking fashion models. So each year designers and magazines should be hiring plainer and plainer girls to model clothes. It'll only be a matter of time before you qualify.

There's not as much money involved in modelling today as there used to be. The knocking down of the Berlin Wall may have been a triumph for freedom but the downside is an influx of beautiful Eastern European women who are happy to work in the West for just a roof over their head and a pair of nylon stockings. My advice would be to forget modelling. It's boring and it destroys your self-esteem.

However, even if you think you have what it takes to make it as a common or garden model you still need to know how to make the transition to famous supermodel.

There is a very distinct difference between a model and a supermodel. You only become a supermodel once you have hired a publicity agent to convince newspapers and magazines to put the word 'supermodel' in front of your name. This simple but crucial distinction can be the difference between earning £200 or £20,000 for the same job.

Once you are a supermodel you are

more than just a mere clothes horse. You are a famous clothes horse, and if your management team has done their job right you're a clothes horse with a personality.

Note: Don't be put off by the personality thing. It won't be yours, it will be created for you.

Punters won't bother to stop and question why a model has been elevated to the status of supermodel, they just accept it. Once you get famous and the punters know you, you can exploit them with as many videos, cookbooks and calendars as you like.

Note: Don't worry if you know nothing about yoga or cooking. Your publisher or production company will put you in touch with experts who will happily do all the thinking and hard work for you. The only thing that will be required from you is a few hours to pose for some pictures for the front cover and the publicity. This is great news as it's the one thing you do well.

The right place to wait around for the right time is probably the Kings Road in Chelsea or London Fashion week. Hang around looking as tall and as pretty as you can manage.

Doctor/Vet

We've already touched on this core skill. The main requirement for a TV or radio doctor or vet is to look handsome and have a good bedside manner. (Don't bother going down this route if you're a female doctor or vet. Housewife viewers won't be interested in your bedside manner.) No knowledge of medicine is actually required, because regardless of what symptoms are presented to you by a patient calling into the show your advice will always be the same. 'Go and see your doctor or vet.' The best way into this is via local radio.

Note: It may be worth becoming formally qualified to avoid any scandals.

The right place to wait for the right time would be a practice near a TV or radio station.

Celebrity journalist

The best route for a journalist to get on TV is landing a job as the TV reviewer. Many TV shows invite reviewers on their programmes to guarantee them at least one good review.

The best way to become a journalist is to practice writing and then, when you are good enough, to bombard the press with what you've written.

The right place to wait for your big break would be in your office, at your desk, writing reviews. Never be too harsh about the shows you could appear in but don't creep either, otherwise they'll have no incentive to invite you on.

Stand-up Comic

You need real balls to get up on stage every night in front of a room full of drunks and tell them jokes. Or so everyone says. It might be a bit nerve-racking the first or second time, but once you've got the hang of it, it's not that difficult. The best way to start is to go and see a lot of comedy in comedy clubs. You'll quickly realise there are certain subjects that always get a laugh from the audience. You need to write your own material on these themes.

There's a simple formula for making people laugh with jokes. First get your audience to picture a probable and plausible situation and then, on the punch line, turn the image in their minds into something that is improbable but still plausible.For example:

'I was sitting in a Happy Eater when a huge big lorry driver came in and said, "Oy you, get outside and give us a push." '

(The image this creates in people's minds is a probable and plausible one.)

'I went outside and he was sat on a swing.'

In the time it takes you to say this four-word punch line, the image in people's minds has been switched to something that is improbable but still plausible. You just have to keep switching the images in your audience's heads like this, to and fro, for about 20 minutes. The more quickly and efficiently you train your audience to make the switch, the funnier the jokes. Talking about emotive subjects like drugs, nostalgia, fear or sex will help keep people interested in you and will help motivate them to make the switch.

There is an exception to this – 'surreal comedy' – where the comic switches the audience from thinking about something plausible and probable to something just stupid. Surreal comedy isn't very good.

If you really want to be a class act then

make your stage persona resonate with your material. So if you are a fat comic, do jokes about eating. If you look like a criminal, talk about robbing banks.

Once you've got enough material written and learned you need to book yourself into some comedy clubs. You'll only be asked to do a five-minute 'open spot' at first and you'll provide this for free. When you get better at what you're doing (ie when you start being funny) you'll start to get paid gigs and be expected to do ten or 20 minutes of comedy. If you can't even get an open spot then set up your own club: all you need is a room in a pub and some posters. Go to a comedy club, ask the comics for their numbers and then offer them a split of the takings if they'll come and perform at your new club. Oh, and don't forget to put yourself on the bill.

The ideal stage to reach for a comic is when you've been on TV a lot and the punters begin to feel that they 'know you'

– they perceive you as an old friend. This is a great place to be because once you've achieved this status you no longer need to be funny any more.

Many TV researchers look for new talent in the comedy clubs of London and with practice and perseverance you will get your big break.

The right place to wait for your big break is on the stage of a comedy club being hilarious.

Actor

This is an unnecessarily tough route to getting famous and it's not for the faint-hearted. Even after you have developed and honed the skills you require (which usually takes three years, after beating some tough competition to get into drama school), you are still required to drag yourself from one casting to the next in the hope that some director thinks you are 'right for the part'.

You will also be up against many actors who, bizarrely, are not interested in getting famous but are driven by The Love Of The Craft. This weird bunch can be very hard to beat as they are usually very committed and 'centred', which is an acting term that means they'll be very good at acting. The average actor is driven partly by lust for fame and partly by love of the craft. If you ask actors what drives them they'll usually tell you that they are driven by love of the craft alone. But behind the scenes they will be busy getting their agents to fight for top billing and instructing their PR offices to get them maximum exposure.

The route to being an actor is more or less this: drama club/amateur drama society, auditioning for stage school, getting an agent and then auditioning and networking for parts.

Auditioning is the main route to success and this is a separate skill from acting. Learning to audition is more important than learning to act. You can be a brilliant actor but if you can't audition you'll starve to death because you never work, whereas if you audition well at least you can learn to get better at acting because you're getting so much experience. The more auditions you do, the better you'll get at doing them.

You have two choices: you can either get good at auditions and get employed and have a nice lifestyle and even get famous or you can bitch about how hit-and-miss the whole audition process is and how it's possible for a director to miss a great actor simply because he's not great at auditions, while you collect glasses in a bar in the West End.

Many out-of-work actors find it useful to have a list of excuses and internal rationalisations as to why they are currently out of a job and on benefits. They think this sets them apart from the other dole pigs at the benefit office. If you would like the complete list of these excuses just listen to the conversations of out-of-work actors in many of the bars and cafés around the casting suites in the West End of London.

Here are some of the other useful techniques that can help you overcome the feeling of low self-esteem and powerlessness when things aren't going your way and you're experiencing long, unhappy periods of unemployment:

Bitching about other more successful actors can be very useful, helping you fake a sense of self-worth.

There are always plenty of courses and **workshops** laid on for professional actors. These will help to create the impression that you are busy, and give you a reason to get up before twelve. They will also save you from the daily grind of having to watch daytime television in your pyjamas.

Marijuana can also be very helpful for filling in the empty void and taking a temporary edge off your unhappiness, although in the long term it will destroy all your drive and ambition and make it harder to learn your lines, and if you're a man it may reduce your testosterone levels and make your dick shrink.

It can be quite tiresome when people ask, 'What have you been up to?' when all you have been up to is smoking dope, looking around record shops and bitching about the Oscar nominees, so a good trick is to start to **write a novel** or a play. You never actually have to finish writing it, as this would take a great deal of effort and would obviously lead to more failure and rejection, so always keep it unfinished. Then you can refer to it in conversations with people who ask you how things are going.

Getting an agent is a must for an out-of-work actor as this will give you something else to bitch about and someone else to blame.

The majority of wannabes who train to be actors will never get famous. Even if they are very successful, without a sustained PR campaign about their tragic personal lives or wonderful love lives they'll always be 'that bloke, you know, the policeman in that country thing with the sixties music ... didn't he leave to be a harbour master?', 'No, he's the one from that soap...'

The same few actors get all the best roles in film and on television because casting directors like to go with what they know. TV and film execs also want to go with 'heritage'. In other words, if they've spent thousands of pounds promoting a certain actor for last year's big production, then they'll want to make the most of this money and use the same actor again for anything else they do, even if there are other actors around who are better or more suitable for the part. They will justify this to their audience with slogans like 'back by popular demand, the return of Britain's best-loved actor'. No one needs to know that he's only popular as a result of all the publicity they spent on him last year and the only reason he's back is to save them having to spend a fortune selling a new actor to the punters.

If you like the idea of having very little control over your destiny, being at the beck and call of casting directors, spending most of your life waiting tables in coffee shops or wearing jogging bottoms, living on the bread line and occasionally picking up a pittance in a 'terribly worthy' production where you don't get paid but you get a share of the door take, then the actor's life is for you.

The right places to wait for the right time? Stage school, Edinburgh festival, London fringe. Don't wait for parts to come to you.

Once you qualify stay active and keep working, even if it's for free. Branch out into writing or directing or stand-up comedy. This way you'll keep your self-esteem high and this will improve your odds in the auditions. The right place to wait for your big break would be in an audition.

TV Chef

If you are going to do this properly the best place to start is catering college. Once you start looking for work, think about the restaurants and cafés where TV folk go to eat. That way you've more chance of being spotted.

It's important that you are comfortable preparing food and presenting to a camera at the same time. Get a video camera on a tripod and practise whenever you get a moment. Get it looking natural. Don't try to copy TV chefs; most of them are irritating, so develop your own style.

Many ovens on TV sets don't work, so it's important that you practise 'this dish is hot' acting. Ten minutes a night in front of the mirror for three months should do the trick.

If you own your own gaff you should offer free meals to the local radio and TV stations. Once you get to know them it will be easier to approach them with ideas for slots in their shows. Make sure you find out who the decision makers are (this can be an impossible task in television, even for someone who has worked in the business for a long time). Don't be too pushy; let the relationship develop naturally. Remember, when they are out for a meal they will have finished work and will be relaxing. The last thing they will want is a wannabe celebrity chef pitching them ideas for new food programmes while they're trying to enjoy themselves.

It's better if you wait for *them* to have the idea, but you can drop a few subtle hints. If they don't offer you anything after a few months then send them the bill for all their food.

The right place to wait for your break would be in a restaurant where media types eat.

Author

You don't have to be an expert to write a book. Just start writing one and by the time you have finished it you will be an expert in your field by virtue of the fact you have written a book on that subject.

Many radio talk shows are desperate for good guests and ideas for shows. They will be very keen for you to come on their show and plug yourself and your book.

It's odd that the Radio Authority and the Independent Television Commission – the authorities that are responsible for ensuring that radio and TV broadcasters are duller than they could be – will allow TV channels shamelessly to give free advertising to authors, actors and musicians but never to any other professions. Not even the ones that produce products that are vital to sustain a healthy way of life such as the manufacturer of peristalsis pumps.

You'd never get the senior mechanic of a peristalsis pump firm appearing on a late night chat show on the eve of the launch of his new peristalsis pump, despite the many advantages such a pump would offer over a conventional pump, such as the ability to pump highly corrosive material. In order to get on to TV and radio talk shows you need to write about something that will appeal to the TV and radio editors.

One excellent title for a book that would get you onto the publicity circuit would be a book on how to get famous (these days television programmes seem to be about little else), especially if such a book made reference to TV talk shows. Your publicist, whose job it is to book you onto this circuit, could point out the relevant chapters in the book that flatter the brilliant and researchers and producers who help to choose which authors get invited on their very entertaining shows.

Radio presenters will also love to have

you on their shows to publicise the book as they will be secretly looking for tips on how to break into television and get more famous themselves.

If you are challenged by the interviewer about the fact that you are not really famous yourself and therefore not qualified to write about the subject, simply ask him if he's read your book. The chances are he won't have. Presenters rarely do. It's the researcher who reads the book and then makes a few brief notes for the presenter. If the presenter has a daily show then he won't have had time to do anything more than skim it. If he's been presenting his show for a while, he won't even have been bothered to do that.

Once you have him on the back foot, explain that your book is an ironic satire on the world of fame and not necessarily a turnkey manual to achieving fame *per se*, although part of the irony lies in the fact that if used as a turnkey manual it would be extremely effective.

You could also point out that it is obvious to anyone who has actually bothered to read the book that the author is far too cynical to be comfortable about getting famous himself, and if he'd bothered to read the biography provided, he would also have noted that the author has been fired from just about every job he has had that could have got him famous.

If you really want to labour the point you can add that a surgeon doesn't need to have heart disease in order to operate on the heart of someone who has. Galileo Galilei didn't actually need to go and visit the sun to work out that the Earth revolved around it. At this point the interview will probably be terminated.

If you do decide to write a book but are worried that you can't write, spell or form proper sentences, just throw some rough ideas down on paper and your editor will rewrite the whole thing for you. Your name still ends up on the front cover in a fancy dot matrix typeface.

The right place to wait for your big break would be either at your computer, writing your next bestseller, or by your front door, waiting to see if your postman is delivering returned manuscripts and rejections or letters of congratulations and contracts. As a general rule of thumb for authors, big packages mean bad news.

Kids' TV Presenter

The competition for children's TV Presenter is very tough so unless your dad was one, or you're very camp, or from an ethnic minority, or have a strong regional accent or a lisp you may as well forget it.

If you still want to go for it, you could start by setting yourself up as a children's entertainer: buy some balloons to make into animals and a few magic tricks. Practise at home and then start to do children's parties for the kids in your family. If you're any good, the word will spread. If you're not any good, video the show, watch it to find out what's wrong with it and lose the bad bits. Once you've got a proper act together, approach holiday parks, seaside resorts or theme parks for a job. This would be a good springboard for you to get into children's television. Once your act is looking good (as good as making animals out of balloons and doing magic tricks can ever get), make a show reel with your video camera and send it off to the kids' channels and to the children's editors on the TV stations. Find out which agents specialise in children's entertainers and send them a copy along with your CV.

By the time you have done a couple of years entertaining kids with your magic show at children's parties and at theme parks, if you still want to work with kids then you're probably mental enough to be able to do the job.

There are genuine rewards and pleasures being a famous children's entertainer that aren't available anywhere else in the world of fame. Children are so young, sweet and innocent and there's so much potential to screw them up psychologically for life. Children are even more gullible than adult punters. Because their minds are not fully developed they will really worship you as a star. You will have their total loyalty and they will believe anything you say.

They also have a lot more free time to watch you on the television and, most importantly these days, they get a lot more pocket money than children ever did before. It doesn't take a great deal of effort to get it off them.

We'll spend more time on cashing in on fame near the end of the book but the potential for milking kids is huge. Not only do advertisers target kids' own money but through 'pester power' they get access to their parents' money too. You'll get your cut through endorsements, public appearances and voice-overs.

The great thing about kids is that they can be made to want any old bit of crap made out of plastic or card so long as it's sold right. The most powerful way to do this is to animate the plastic and card in an advert so that the thing 'comes to life'. Once the kids get their own version home it'll look just like a bit of old plastic and card again but you won't need to worry about this as you will already have been paid.

Get kids when they are young and you'll have them in your fan base for the rest of your working life. When they are teenagers they will go through a stage of hating you but in their late teens and early twenties they will like you again in an ironic way. If you can make the switch to presenting for adults you'll have established a fan base or, as it's known in the business, heritage.

How to get out of Children's TV

Like most children's presenters your main concern once you've got your first job will be how to get out and make the crossover into adult TV before you get to old and it begins to look dirty. The older you get in children's television the dirtier it looks.

The best way for girls to 'mature' their image is to flash their paler bits in the mens' style magazines. However this route is not recommended for the boys. The most effective and sure way for male children's presenters to mature their image is to be caught taking drugs or having sex. After the initial feigned shock from the rest of the media, industry producers will start to consider you for more adult jobs, especially if you can put them in touch with your dealer.

Reality TV Show Contestant

I'm not really sure that there are any skills required to be a reality TV show contestant, unless having an 'outgoing personality' is a skill. One thing you have to make sure of is that your personality clashes with the other contestants' personalities.

These shows are very successful because they appeal to the punters' very worst instincts for salacious gossip and voyeurism. However, to make the punters feel better about wasting their lives watching 12 other punters wasting theirs, the TV companies often call the shows 'social experiments'. This gives the whole thing an air of respectability

As this book went to print, no major advancements or breakthroughs in modern science have been facilitated by these 'experiments'.

By all means go along to the auditions and take your chances but this is a hit-and-miss way of getting famous and the odds are already heavily stacked against you, even if you are as camp as a house and have a 'bubbly' personality and a quirky regional accent. You'll look down the queue waiting for your chance to shine and discover that maybe you're not as unique as you thought you were. You'll find the queue full of people who are just as annoying, all claiming to be a 'little bit mad', whose mates all think that they are really funny and should be on telly.

As more and more of these shows appear on our television sets, the time contestants spend being famous once the shows are over decreases. One or two survive but they are usually the ones with good core skills. Fewer and fewer shows are tending to book reality TV contestants and eventually the only places you will end up are talk shows entitled 'I was a reality TV game show contestant'.

The best place to wait for your big break will be listed in the latest edition of *The Stage* and *Television Today*. All open auditions will be in there. Good luck.

Serial Killer

Becoming a vile serial killer will get you famous but there are a couple of drawbacks to think about before you reach for the axe and the gaffer tape.

In order to really make it big as a vile serial killer you need to get caught. You shouldn't see this as a sign of weakness but as an opportunity. Once you get caught you will achieve what many wannabes can only dream about – instant worldwide fame.

Once you're caught, newspapers will be falling over themselves in the rush to be the first to publish your picture. If you have been on the run for a while you will undoubtedly get on to the front pages of most of the nationals and then everyone will be able to put a face to a name. As a bonus, you'll get an opportunity to use your real name and not just the one the boys in the police incident room have chosen for you (although you might prefer to keep your police name as it can often add mystique, glamour and credibility to your vile actions).

It may be necessary to add a word of caution here. The coverage you get in the papers as a vile serial killer might not be entirely favourable. Some newspapers editors have a very low view of sick and violent criminals and you may get the kind of hostile treatment usually reserved for last year's winner of a TV reality game show.

There tends to be a bias in favour of the victims whenever a newspaper covers vile serial killers, which often amounts to a PR disaster for the criminal. (Fortunately, this bias is completely reversed in our justice system.)

Despite the modern world's very liberal attitude to criminals there is very little opportunity to cash in on your new-found fame. Public appearances are difficult to arrange from inside jail and in any event, even if you manage to arrange leave or escape, supermarket bosses tend to prefer someone from a soap or an Olympic medallist to cut the ribbon.

Having said that, there is an exception to this rule. If you're from the East End of London it won't matter how evil or immoral you are or what crimes you have committed. As long as you love your mum and you only butchered your own you should get a book deal and get to do the chat show circuit on your release. No one is sure why this is. Maybe it's because as a nation we're not so bothered about cockneys getting killed.

The best place to wait for your big break is in some bushes after dusk.

MP

If you prefer talking to doing, and lying comes as second nature to you, why not consider becoming an MP? You will quickly achieve national fame because TV companies have to feature MPs prominently in the news in order to protect their licence or charter, which is controlled by MPs. How long do you think the BBC would last if they put a blanket ban on MPs in their news?

If you do get elected and make it into government you stand a really good chance of extending your fame world-wide. One of the ways to this is to engineer a war. Not only will this guarantee you a place in the history books but it will ensure you'll never have to worry about fulfilling any of your promises on domestic policy, as you can always claim you have more important things to think about than the job you were elected to do.

It's not really important which political party you join as long as they stand a good chance of getting into government. Try and judge the political mood of the time before you make a decision one way or another. It can be difficult to change parties once you have joined one, but it's not impossible.

The best course of action is to find out

which party normally gets into power in your area and join that one. If your local MP is young and popular then it might be a good idea to move constituencies. Ideally you want a popular MP who is about to retire or die.

Don't think too hard about policy or ideas – these are just window-dressing in modern politics. What's vital is simply persuading the punters that you are the man for the job. It's more important to convince people you can get things done than it is actually to get anything done. It may be necessary to get the occasional thing done to win back the confidence of the electorate but don't let this sidetrack you from your main job of *appearing* to get things done. This is what wins elections. There's no point getting anything done at all if you then lose the next election because you haven't appeared to get anything done. The joy of parliament is that it's a great alternative to the drugs, alcohol or homeless shelters where most of the losers in life end up.

If you couldn't get a teaching certificate, don't worry, you can become minister for education. You may have failed to get into the TA, but that won't stop you working in the defence department and running the army. And if you didn't make it as a rock star, it's not a problem – thousands will be chanting your name at party conferences.

And more importantly, without needing any real skills you will get famous. You will end up writing books, sitting on the boards of big companies and appearing on TV and radio.

Given the variety of window-lickers and perverts thats end up in the House of Commons, you can see that if you have half a brain and don't scare children too much you are already way ahead of most of the people who are successful in this field.

It is important that I issue a word of warning though. Becoming an MP is not for the honest or anyone with ideals or principles. You must get rid of any notion you may have of wanting to save the world or do any good. Save that talk for the punters at the elections and for the party faithful at the conferences, but don't believe a word of it yourself. You will only be a successful MP if you use it as a selfish vehicle to achieve your own fame, wealth and success. You're not going to make the world a better place; in fact, if history is anything to go by, you are going to make it much worse. But don't worry – the world's loss is your gain. You must lose any honesty or idealistic tendencies you have, otherwise these weaknesses will be exploited by your enemies and used against you.

It's no coincidence that the one word that is not allowed to be used in the House of Commons is 'liar'. You may think it's odd that any word can be banned from use in the very seat of freedom and democracy, let alone this one, but it is banned for a very good reason. Lying will be your main method of survival and success as a politician. If the word were permitted in parliament it would be the most used word in the house with the possible exception of 'you', 'dirty' and 'little'.

Honesty loses to dishonesty every time in politics. Imagine if in the Olympics you were not allowed to use the words 'drug', 'taking' or 'cheat' and no one was allowed to be tested for performance-enhancing drugs. The honest athlete who holds the ideals of the Olympic code sacred simply could not compete with the hundreds of competitors who would be happy to get doped up to the eyeballs, knowing they'd never get caught. There are obviously the odd exceptions, but these can be counted on the fingers of one hand of a man who's had a nasty industrial accident in a bacon-slicing factory.

It's not difficult to see why you would lose if you were to stand for election honestly. Regardless of your politics, if you were obeying the rules of complete honesty, you would say that if people wanted better public services then they would have to pay more tax. Or that if they wanted to pay less in tax then public services should be downscaled.

What people want is for public services to increase and for themselves to pay less tax. So if some dishonest candidate comes along and promises just that, he's going to beat you hands down. The punters know that all politicians are liars, so they are just as likely to believe the bloke making false promises as they are you – and he's got a message they like, so you lose. Eventually you will learn your lesson and realise that the only way you are going to win is by becoming the more convincing liar. You can justify the lies to yourself by saying things like 'the end justifies the means' and 'when we're in government we will change things for the better'. What you don't count on is that power is a drug, and the more you get the more you want and the only way to get more is to lie more.

The best place to wait for the right time is in your local political club, lying like a trooper.

Student

Universities can offer many ways into the life of fame. First of all, you can practise most of the core skills you need to get famous in a relatively friendly and safe environment away from the scary real world. Most universities have radio stations, TV studios, theatres, comedy nights and even elections for the student union.

If you go to Oxford or Cambridge you are more likely to be able to network with the movers and shakers of the future TV and radio industry, but if you're too thick or your father can't afford to bribe the admissions tutor then there are still networking opportunities at other colleges.

For example, you could take part in a work experience programme as part of a media studies degree. You will usually get a job placement as a runner in your holidays or your year out. Make sure it's with a big company in London, and then work hard and network like crazy. The actual degree will be of little value in comparison to the value you will get from this networking.

Note: If you do end up applying for a media studies degree, make a note to yourself to ignore everything that your tutor tells you about the world of media, regardless of what job he tells you he used to have in television. Also don't put down that you want to be famous on your application form. Competition is already very tight for places on these course so there is little to be gained from shooting yourself in the foot before you get an interview.

Cult Leader

If you're finding it difficult to make it into society's mainstream entertainment indus-tries then why not create your own society by forming a cult? It may take a while to get started, but it will be well worth the effort because amongst your own members you will be worshipped as a god here on earth, which can be a very rewarding and enjoyable experience.

Here are a couple of ideas to attract people to your cult:

Immortality. People don't like the idea that one day they'll die and then that'll be it, so if you can offer some kind of ever-lasting life people will bite your hand off.

Easy sex is a great sales pitch and has worked over many years for organisations like the Mormons and Club 18-30 holidays. Cults like Catholicism attracted a great many people by making sex much harder, but since they stopped burning non-believers their popularity has waned. Easy sex tends to attract men more than women. This is because women tend to be able to get sex much more easily than men

– as long as they are prepared to drop their standards low enough.

Once you have hooked members into joining your cult you can start to manipulate them. Guilt is a great way to do this. It's not difficult to manipulate punters with guilt. The techniques invented to create guilt haven't changed since it was introduced as a device to control punters just over two thousand years ago. To make punters feel guilty you need to convince them that their perfectly normal emotions, desires and feelings are evil and wrong.

Once this has been achieved, each time your followers feel these things they will experience guilt. Then you step in with some kind of absolution to ease their guilt, or if you're feeling really mischievous, some kind of punishment for feeling these 'bad emotions'. Most cult leaders prefer a mixture of the two; the old carrot and the stick gets the maximum results every time.

Another great scam you can pull is not to promise immortality unconditionally;

make sure the punters jump through a few hoops for you first. If you make sure that they can only achieve eternal salvation through you then you are going to get the most value out of each of your members.

Here's a handy tip: If you make total obedience one of the hoops then you'll end up with a lot more leeway to change your mind about what kind of things you want your followers to do for you in the future.

If you follow these simple guidelines, you'll get loads of people running around after you answering your every whim. This is the kind of thing that many stars and celebrities fight long and hard to get put in their contracts.

The Reluctant Producer Scam

This is a tried and tested method for getting in front of the camera. Once you have moved up the ranks from runner to producer or researcher using the techniques we outlined earlier. You can also use this method to get one of your friends on to TV.

As a producer or researcher, sooner or later you will be charged with the task of finding the on-air talent for the TV show you are working on. This is because the media is obsessed with finding new and young talent despite the fact that the industry is awash with very experienced and capable talent.

(Luckily, this is one of the few industries that work like this. Imagine being told by your nurse during your pre-medical that your heart and lung transplant is to be carried out by some bright, raw talent whom the hospital has found in an open talent contest, rather than the experienced but 'stale' senior surgeon they fired inorder to freshen things up a bit.)

Initial auditions for TV presenters are usually carried out by a researcher or producer who has no involvement in making the final decision. Often this fact is kept from the wannabe presenter so that the researcher can enjoy the feeling of power for the first time in his life. The auditions are recorded on to tape and then sent to the executives who actually make the decisions.

If you are just such a researcher looking for your own slice of fame, you must conduct extensive but half-hearted auditions. If possible leave the best candidates off the tape or, better still, give them a slightly false brief so they don't look so good.

For example, if the senior executive is a big fan of the interactive part of the show and its use of email, you could encourage the wannabe presenters to take the mickey out of the internet. You will find they are eager to please you and will be happy to say any line you suggest. You can use this effectively to eliminate them from the race.

You will be asked to keep auditioning people until the deadline to find your new presenter approaches. If you continue to search for people in the way described, eventually panic will set in as the executives start to get desperate.

With only a few days to go before the show goes into production you should reluctantly offer to audition or suggest one of your friends. At this stage the producers have nothing to lose. You will already be familiar with the brief and know exactly how the executives want it filled. So your chances of success are very high.

This scam has launched many successful careers and is still being put to good use today.

The flip side to this is that if you have been called for an audition and you are not best mates with the researcher then your chances of success are very low. To avoid getting into this situation I suggest you read and put into practice the tips on networking later in this book.

FAQ from female wannabes

I am often approached by women who come to me seeking advice on how to get famous, and it's true that there are techniques and issues regarding getting famous that only apply to women. In this chapter I have listed and answered a few of the most frequent questions that I have been asked.

Q: How do I get my kit off in a men's style magazine while still being respected for what I do? (Even if most of what I do is getting my kit off in men's style magazines?)

A: Gentlemen's and lads' style magazines are a recent phenomenon. Fifteen years ago, the only magazines exclusively for men were hardcore porn mags. These often had a couple of articles about gadgets, cars or bikes in them but were mainly bought because of the pictures of naked women.

These magazines took a certain amount of courage to buy. The best technique was to go to a quiet newsagent's and slip the magazine into a copy of another newspaper – usually a highbrow one like *The Times* or *Guardian*. This would often backfire when the newsagent couldn't find the price on the mag at just about the same time as your neighbour arrived in the shop with her two young children and you would be exposed as a red-faced pervert.

These days all that embarrassment has been removed with the introduction of mens' style magazines. They have a lot more articles about gadgets, cars or bikes in them but are still mainly bought for the pictures of naked women. They're the new wave of respectable jazz mags. Men no longer feel ashamed to be seen with them in public.

They're also a great shop window for female presenters and actresses who want to get in or stay in the limelight. You will have to be prepared to take your clothes off, but your picture will always be accompanied by an article for the men to read. This helps them and you to feel less dirty.

There are certain DO's and DONT'S that will help you exploit these magazines and the men who read them:

When you pose DO remember that this isn't Razzle or a medical journal. So DON'T show pink bits, only show white bits. (Or lighter bits if you are of ethnic origin.)

DON'T allow yourself to be photographed down on all fours, no matter how tasteful the photographer says it will look with his special lighting and soft focus filter lens.

DON'T hold or touch any of your body parts, although it is permissible to use the side of your arm to create a cleavage or your hands to cover your breasts.

DO drape something over half of your backside to disguise its true size.

DO make sure that the photograph is artistically shot and beautifully lit so that at a later date when you get questioned on a chat show about your nudity you can say 'well, it was artistically shot and beautifully lit'. For the icing on the cake, say 'and as you know, Carl is a great photographer'. It doesn't matter whether he is or not. If you only use his Christian name people will just assume they should know who he is.

DO, when interviewed, say something that is sexy without being dirty. This will be the quote that the magazine will highlight in bold to get the punters' interested in the interview and in you.

It won't matter what you say in this interview because, if necessary in the future, you can always deny you made these comments or claim that they were taken out of context. Here are some examples of sexy things to say during your interview.

I've always dreamed of doing it with a perfect stranger.

This is a great quote as it makes the reader think he's actually in with a chance. Never say you would actually *like* to have sex with a stranger, as this would make you seem a little bit desperate for sex. Men find desperate women less attractive.

Never say that you have actually *had* sex with a perfect stranger either, as this will make you appear like a cheap tart. The idea is to titillate without sounding like you're writing a confession for a top- shelf magazine.

Sex outside has always excited me.

This is good, but never say you actually like to have sex outside, otherwise whenever you leave your home you'll never be more than 500 yards away from a photographer's long lens.

All I really want is a man to love me all day.

Don't say this. It puts too much pressure on the reader and will make them feel inadequate and exhausted at the thought.

I like it hard and nasty.

No, this is very wrong.

A very popular technique of appearing flirty is to talk about the first time you ever made love. This kind of sex talk is appealing as it has an innocence and sweetness to it. If your first time was a terrible sordid and painful affair then it would be best not to mention it or make something up.

Q: Is hardcore porn a viable route to mainstream fame?

A: Although one or two stars (male and female) from soft-core films have made it big in Hollywood, as yet no hardcore glamour model has ever made a successful switch to the mainstream and so it's not a route I'd recommend, unless you are planning a career in Italy where hardcore queens can even get elected to parliament.

Times are changing and the hardcore industry is becoming more acceptable, but for now, if your boyfriend tries to convince you that you'll get famous by sending some pictures to the amateur section of his favourite adult magazine, my advice would be to resist the temptation, no matter how much the £25 payment might appeal to you.

Admittedly some soldiers or truckers might pin you up in their lockers but most of your pictures will be found soiled under a hedge or in a graveyard by some school boys.

In any event the amateur sections of such magazines are only for women who like to pose nude but can't make it into the regular pages of the magazine on account of their lazy eye or hare-lip.

Q: What options are open to me if I'm ugly?

A: Like it or not, sex sells and if you're a woman without sex appeal then you're in trouble.

Let's face facts: how many ugly, famous women are there? I don't care how many you think there *should* be. Maybe there should be more ugly women on our televisions and in our magazines; maybe you should start a campaign to get more ugly people on the TV. This in itself could get you famous, but you'd always be the ugly nut that gets wheeled out when programme-makers are short of ideas.

There are very few outlets for the ugly, so unless your dad is a top producer of American TV programmes there's not a lot you can do. Plastic surgery might be the answer but even then you must remember that surgeons are only human and can't perform miracles. They can only work with the material they've got.

You may feel that my advice is harsh but I'm telling you this for your own good. It's bad enough you being ugly without wasting your life chasing something that's never going to happen. Embrace reality and go and get a job where you're not seen.

You may be clinging to the notion that beauty's only skin deep but unfortunately cameras can't see past skin. So unless one of the celebrity magazines is planning a special edition of x-rays of the world's ugliest stars and their beautiful homes you're going to be out of luck.

Ugly people can still become writers, radio presenters and character actors.

Ugly women used to get a lot of work as the butt of jokes in comedies, but the latest trends for political correctness have meant that this is no longer the case and many of these women are now out of work or dead. It can still be possible to make fun of ugly people if it is done in an ironic way.

If you've got a really offensive face then you can always become a newspaper critic. After all, if you can't have a career of your own in show business why not make it your career to bitch about other people's?

Q: I'm a teenage girl. Are there any special tricks I can use to help make it?

A: A great technique that is only really open to the teenage girl is to launch your career aged 14 or 15 in a school uniform or a thick jumper, and then once you turn 16 release your second album wearing only a G-string and a snake. This is known as the Lolita factor.

This Lolita factor can help to broaden your appeal right across the family. The school kids love you because you're one of them, but dad takes a keen interest also. Everyone's happy, with the possible exception of mum. Only try this approach if you're a young teenage girl and remember to stay close to your mum.

Note: If you are afraid of snakes why not use a small crocodile or a spider?

As an added bonus, if you decide to go the Lolita route, why not pretend to be a virgin? Obviously don't really be one, as it's not worth it. If you have a virginal image mum will warm to you, the press will be fascinated with you and dad will be even more frustrated by you. It will also help you tap into the lucrative right-wing Christian market. Who knows, you may even get to meet the Pope before he dies.

Word of caution: If you have a show-biz rock star boyfriend and you claim to be a virgin he will be a laughing-stock across most of the western world, although only people in parts of America will actually believe you anyway.

When you finally split with your boyfriend and he reveals that you've been at it like rabbits for years it will make sensational copy and great publicity for you especially, if he had the foresight to take pictures.

Q: I want to sleep with a star to get famous. Where do I find one?

A: The best places to pick up stars is in London, in the West End nightclubs. If you have problems getting to London why not seek out a married premiership footballer in your local city? Despite the large numbers of footballers who have been caught in kiss- and-tell stories by the press, it is still possible for an attractive woman (ideally a blonde with big breasts) to pick up a footballer. You can usually find him in a lap dancing club, from where you'll be able to take him back to yours, shag him and then call the Sunday papers the next day to get a double picture spread.

When you are interviewed always claim you were the innocent party seduced by his fame and money. This way you will get the sympathy and everyone will think that he took advantage of you.

Try and seek out a married player for maximum press coverage. The downside about this technique is that, although it always works, even with good core skills it will be difficult to convert this kind of fame into something longer-lasting. You will probably only get a couple of days' worth of exposure per player at best.

Getting noticed

Once you've learned the skills or set of skills that are going to be your ticket to getting famous, then it's time to sell yourself. You will have to sell yourself not only to the general public but also to the people who are in a position to offer you the kind of work that will get you famous. Depending on what skills you have chosen these could be club promoters, radio station bosses, head chefs or TV researchers. Everything in the Fame Game starts with networking.

Networking

Networking has been given a bad name and net-workers are often sneered at and made to feel very cheap and shallow. This is great news, as networking is one of the most effective tools there is for becoming successful and so it's important that as few people as possible feel comfortable using it.

The more people that feel guilty about networking, the smaller the competition. Many losers or 'neverbes' even feel superior about not networking. This is good news for the rest of us.

There aren't enough hours in the day to network with enough people for you to become famous by networking alone, so what you need to do is concentrate on networking with the people who can offer you the kind of work that can get you famous.

Do you remember the phrase, 'It's not what you know, it's who you know?' Or whom you know? Well, it's through networking that you get to know the who(m)s.

There is an art to successful networking. If you can't do it well, you're better off not doing it at all. If you do it badly you end up looking crass and this will do you a great deal more harm than good. You don't want all the who-you-knows, knowing that you are a greasy, arse-licking slime ball. So here are a few simple tips:

Be yourself and be honest; don't lie about your interests just to have something in common with your new best friend. Instead, look for genuine points of common interest and talk about those.

Ask questions and listen to the answers carefully. People love talking about themselves so they will end up liking you more and you will learn a great deal about them and their business. This will make it easier for you to plan how you can fit into their business.

Be patient and take your time. When you network with a new contact, don't give them a sales pitch on the first meeting, just get to know them. Remember the story of the tortoise and the hare and apply it's meaning to this situation.

Remember the golden rule of getting famous: Never tell anyone you want to get famous.

Publicity

Twenty-five years ago you could have done a five-minute spot on a TV talent show and got famous overnight with hardly any publicity.

These days, with hundreds of TV channels to choose from, more and more radio stations and competition from Multiplex cinemas and the internet, just getting on the television or being in the movies isn't enough to get famous. You need to back it up with lots of publicity.

It's the publicity that turns the actor, chef or presenter into a household name. Without the backup in the press, you're just that bloke off the telly. The presenter of an antiques show only really becomes a famous antiques presenter when you've read about his trauma as a child in the tabloids and looked around his beautiful home in the glossy magazines.

To really permeate into the public consciousness you need total saturation and this is something you won't get unless you have an enormous amount of money behind you.

Contacting the Press Yourself

For the press to be interested in you before you are famous you need to be involved in an amazing story. So if you haven't been in an amazing story then get involved in one soon. Have a look at the kind of stories that make it into the papers and do something similar. Ask yourself, 'What does the editor of this newspaper think his readers like to read about?' If your newspaper is full of stories about courageous animals then buy a dog with three legs and get it to save your life.

Just sending a press release about yourself to the editor of a newspaper won't work. The amount of promotional material that crosses a magazine editor's or TV producer's desk is tremendous and to crack this market on your own is an almost impossible task. The journalists will tend to take the easy option and get their show business stories from publicity agents they trust. So initially my advice would be to start with smaller, more local publications.

You could create the impression you have a PR agency working for you simply by using a printer, a computer and a friend. Print your friend's name, address and number as a letterhead, then type out your story. Get your friend to act as your PR agent, liaise with the newspapers and arrange an interview.

If you don't have a friend maybe you could act as your own publicity agent by experimenting with different voices.

Only contact the press when you have something to sell, like tickets for a gig or a book. The newspapers will only do a story on you a few times a year at most and so you have to make sure you can cash in on it when they do. The smart stars only ever do publicity when they want to flog something. That way they don't risk the public getting bored with them in between projects.

If you need help making up a story, here's some inspiration. It's a real example: one of the many faked stories you will find pretending to be news every day in your newspapers.

It's about a female radio DJ posing for a gentleman's style magazine and was fabricated simply to get publicity for the DJ *and* the radio station *and* the magazine.

The headline for this article was 'DJ IN A SPIN'. This is the required tabloid headline for any articles about DJs. It's journalist law.

In this particular example, the headline 'DJ IN A SPIN' is next to a picture of the nearly naked female DJ posing in a bath tub, and the rest of the article goes on to explain how this particular nearly naked DJ's bosses were shocked and furious when they bought a copy of the men's style magazine only to find their employee splashed across the centre pages nearly naked. They immediately jumped to the conclusion that she must have had the photos taken on a day off when she was supposed to be at home with the flu and they are now considering sacking her.

When you read between the lines of this article you immediately smell a rat. No boss of a radio station would be furious to find one of his DJs nearly naked in a men's style magazine. His immediate response would be, 'Wow, what great publicity – why didn't we think of that?'

Plus, if they are the kind of men to be shocked by a nearly naked lady then what were they doing buying a mens style magazine in the first place?

Additionally, it's not possible to tell when a picture was taken simply by looking at it. Her bosses couldn't have guessed that it was taken on the day she was supposed to have flu and so they have no grounds to sack her.

Any tabloid editor would have spotted that this was a fake story. However, they would have printed it anyway because they'll never pass up the opportunity to reprint a picture of a nearly naked lady.

The magazine was happy to allow the newspaper to publish its picture of a nearly naked lady in return for a plug.

The radio station gets two lots of publicity – one in the magazine and one in the newspaper.

The nearly naked lady also gets to raise her profile.

One thing the article didn't mention was that the radio station and the magazine are both owned by the same media company. I won't mention the name of the radio station as they have had enough publicity out of this sham already. However, you won't be surprised to learn that, four months later, the female DJ hasn't been sacked.

Once you start to read between the lines of show business stories like this you will get a better understanding of how fake the fame game is and you will feel more comfortable with faking it yourself.

You must learn to see through the fakes because the more in tune you are with the reality of show business, the greater your chances of success. As a rule of thumb don't take anything at face value in the papers – dig a little deeper to look at the story behind the paper's version.

Your best bet as you take your first steps to fame is to leave the newspapers alone for now and look at alternative methods of getting publicity. It *is* possible to generate publicity without an agent. Be creative and think laterally. Many bands and even some movies have broken through to the mainstream by means of alternative, low-budget marketing methods including using the internet – so it is possible.

The Traps

There are a great many traps and pitfalls that wannabes fall into as they try to reach their goal of getting famous. Here are just a few of them.

Public Mass Auditions

The mass public audition is one of the oldest cons in the book. In the old days, the circus would come to town, put up a few posters and approach the local newspaper for a mention. The newspaper would reply, 'No way! If you want to advertise in our paper you're going to have to pay for it like everyone else.'

So, as you have learned and as the circus people realised all that time ago, the best way to get publicity in the papers is to invent some 'news' that the editor thinks his readers will be interested in. And so the mass audition con was born.

Whenever the circus arrived in town

they'd always be 'short of a couple of clowns' and so they'd hold 'public auditions'. Everyone in the town would get excited, queues would form for the auditions and the newspapers would always be there to cover it. They'd often send along a journalist to audition and then write about his experiences. However, somewhere in the queue of locals would be two strangers who happened to be experts at throwing custard pies and falling over. In every town the same two jokers would turn up and always get the gig.

This con is as old as the hills but it's still being used today by pop groups and theatre productions. In fact, entire TV shows are built around the mass audition idea and the publicity it generates sells tons of records and concert tickets.

So when your favourite pop group announces that it's holding open auditions to replace one of its members:

★ Don't get too excited about the prospect of auditioning.

★ Just stop and use your loaf for a second. Put yourself in the position of the pop group's manager.

★ If you wanted to replace a band member of a successful chart-topping band with someone who needs to be able to sing and dance to a professional standard and who has touring and recording experience ... where would you look?

Would you:

★ Use your extensive contacts and ask agents, producers and other artists to provide you with a list of the best backing singers and dancers available?

★ Go to the graduation shows of the top theatre and dance schools to have a look at the latest trained dancers and voices?

★ Give up your weekend and get in your car to drive 180 miles to see what raw talent you can in a church hall in Scunthorpe?

Agents

One of the biggest traps you can get caught in is believing that it's your agent's responsibility to get you work – it isn't. You mustn't rely on your agent for this. You need to generate your own work.

So now you're wondering, 'If I shouldn't rely on an agent to get me any work, what's the point of having one and why should I pay them a cut of my cash?'

Well, no one will take you seriously if you don't have an agent. They are the first port of call for any casting director, researcher or producer looking for an act. These people will very rarely deal with an act who hasn't got an agent, although one or two of them will try and deal with you directly and bypass your agent if they want to screw you over.

Agents are seen as filters for TV researchers looking for talent. The good agents have already done most of the legwork finding the best of the talent. That isn't to say there are a lot of talentless acts with agents and a lot of talented acts without agents.

It can be tricky knowing which kind of agent to approach when you're starting out in show business. Obviously, you need one who's experienced in selling your kind of skills, so if you want to be a TV chef then the agents you send your CV off to should at least have one or two TV chefs on their books.

One dilemma you will have to face when choosing an agent is this. Do you approach the big swanky agents with the offices in the West End of London with all the top stars on their books? Or do you try and get in with a smaller agent, maybe one in Cheadle, who looks after some 'lesser-known' people like that bloke who reads the news on Granada Plus at the weekends and on bank holidays?

The benefits of being a little act in a big agency is that you will often get a few tit-bits thrown your way from the bigger acts' table. Swanky agents can use the power of their big acts to crowbar their little acts into supporting roles and thereby build up their profile.

The guests and presenters on TV shows and the stars in magazines are not always the first choice of the celebrity bookers, producers or editors. Less popular celebrities can be forced onto shows by aggressive agents. For example, if an agent has a very popular celebrity whom a TV producer wants for a show, he will get some of his less well-known acts on the show as well, by only offering his big star acts as part of a package deal. He will say:

'If you want to book this top star for your show, you'll also have to take these two talentless wannabes and this old has-been. Otherwise, the deal is off.'

This way his other stars start to get the vital exposure they need to become popular in their own right. Once they're getting on TV regularly, other producers, researchers and celebrity bookers will want them on their shows because they've seen them on telly.

The downside of having a swanky agent is that you will get very frustrated that that agent is spending most of his or her time on the acts that are making the money and putting the kids through college and not on you. After all, it takes about the same amount of time to take a call for a £200 booking as it does for £20,000 one.

The ideal situation, of course, is to be a big act with a big powerful agent but you have to start somewhere.

Getting a smaller agent will avoid this problem but being a bigger fish in a smaller pond also has its drawbacks. You may get the lion's share of your agent's time, but the chances are your agent will be rubbish. Otherwise they'd have some big acts on their books.

Also, be careful about agents who have hundreds of acts on their books. They won't need you to work very much in order for them to make a living. All their acts could be on a tiny annual income and the agency wouldn't be bothered because it's taking a tiny slice of lots of people's fees.

One way of getting an agent is by contacting them when you get a job and asking them if they'll negotiate the deal for you. They are more likely to be interested because they can see you're getting work and they can see themselves getting cash up front.

You will have to pay your agent a percentage of your income, which can vary from between 10 and 15 per cent. Some 'artistes' prefer a manager to an agent. Managers tend to charge 20 per cent. The main difference between a manager and an agent is that a manager is an agent who charges an extra 5 per cent.

Very few agents will be proactive. Some

managers might be a little more hands-on. Some of the more successful agents (i.e. those that control some of the more successful stars) can control more of the game. In the main, agents will sift through the briefs they get from production companies, suggest you for anything you 'look right for' and then wait to hear whether you've got it. Then they will negotiate the price for you. Often they can get as much as 10 or 15 per cent extra for a deal, which is great as it will nearly cover their fee.

Living the Dream

Sustaining your fame with PR

Some religious fundamentalists believe that if a homosexual man puts his trust in Jesus it is possible through the power of prayer for him to turn back into a 'normal' heterosexual. However, the most effective way for a gay man to turn straight is not through Jesus but through his PR agent.

It may come as a shock to you but many men in the world of show business actually like to have sexual relationships with other men. Despite what you might think, gay men have no problems finding work in the theatre, television and film industries. What might be harder for some people to comprehend is that these men feel the need to hide their sexuality from their fans.

Since Ancient Greek times some of mankind's most powerful and brilliant movers and shakers from the worlds of arts, science and entertainment have been homosexual, and yet, all these years on, gay men in the public eye still feel they have to pretend they are straight. Many a star believes that if his fans found out he was homosexual they would be broken-hearted and would stop being fans.

This would probably only be true in cases where a gay star has projected a false straight image to build up a fan base of straight women. Whether you are a gay or straight performer, one of the best ways to get the best out of your punters is to tease and lead them on into believing they might be in with a chance of romance with you, 'if only the conditions were right'. (Eg If they were alone on the beach and the moon was shining in a bright mid-summer sky and the fan wasn't a 45-year-old overweight, meno-pausal moose from Crewe.) This vague hope in the back of the punter's mind could be her main motivation for following you around from concert to concert buying your T-shirts, calendars and CDs.

If the punters found out you were gay it could break the love spell you've cast upon them, and that might just bring them to their senses.

To create the illusion of heterosexuality for you, therefore, the PR agent will arrange for you to have a 'beard'. This is the term for a pretend girlfriend or wife who is designed to make a homosexual man appear more manly. The 'beard' usually will be another of your PR agent's clients. It's a win-win situation. The relationship will generate plenty of publicity in its own right, and if your 'beard' is a very attractive model, then this will boost your star status. On the other hand, if you're already a well-known name then this could be the boost the model needs to make the leap from model to supermodel.

All you will need to do to fake a relationship is have some photographs taken while kissing your new love. These are usually taken with a long lens so it looks as though you are unaware of the photographers and are just enjoying a private moment. Other than this, you will be required to go to a few premieres and show business parties together and be seen entering and leaving certain restaurants together. If you want to be photographed for the papers, then these are the restaurants you must go to. If you want a quiet night out with your lover without your spouse knowing, then it is often a good idea to avoid these restaurants. To many this might seem like obvious advice but you'll be surprised how many famous people don't follow it. When you want to be left alone there are plenty of nice restaurants in Oldham you can go to.

Fake relationships aren't only arranged for homosexuals. So if you are a heterosexual, don't worry. You too can have relationships created for you whenever you have a new album or TV series to flog to the punters.

How to deal with bad press

If you court the press they will see you as their property and one day, unless you are a total saint and nothing has ever gone wrong in your life, they will turn on you. Even if you are a total saint they'll dig and dig until they can find nothing to make something out of.

The press trot out the same old justification for intruding into people's private lives which helps them sleep at night and keeps the punters and authorities off their backs. The justification goes like this:

> 'You invited the press into your life in the first place when you wanted publicity for your single/TV show/film etc. So what do you expect? Of course we're going to hound you every single day of the week from now on, follow you on your holidays and take photos of you with a long lens.'

I don't understand the logic. If you invite people round for dinner one evening to celebrate the birth of your child or a promotion at work, would this give them the impression that they could arrive at your home any day of the week from then on and demand to be fed or even camp outside on your drive waiting for titbits or rummaging through your bins?

When your private life is intruded into by the press, you will be left in no doubt as to how wrong this is. However, there is nothing you can do about it. It is simply the nature of the beast. The press are a little like vampires. They can't usually harm you unless you invite them into your home.

The PR Disaster

When the press have caught you with your pant down, wipe the slate clean with a tell-all confession that'll get the public back on your side and loving you even more. Explain how you've learnt your lesson and how you have changed.

This scam only usually works once, so it's important that you're much more careful not to get caught the next time.

Once you have got famous by following the advice in this book, and once you have built up an army of punters to be milked with merchandise, books and videos etc, newspaper editors will cotton on to your ability to shift product. They will begin to look for stories on you so that you can sell their newspapers.

Newspapers will often hang on to dirt they have on you and only release it to the public when that dirt can have the maximum impact. Newspapers don't always print the news as it happens, they print it when it's going to sell the most papers.

For example, if you become a pop star and end up having a three-in-the-bed romp with the wife and daughter of a government minister and the papers find out about it ... the chances are they will hold on to the story until either you are ready to release your new single or the minister is up for re-election. Ideally, both.

This way the story will ride on the top of all the publicity your PR agent will already be generating, which will make it much bigger news. And while they're sitting on the story, the papers will normally drop a few hints to your press office that they have the story to ensure that they get your maximum cooperation with other matters.

Often newspapers will save a story if they have other news to print that week. They only really need one big scoop per edition, so if they get two scoops on one day they can happily save one of their scoops for tomorrow's news.

There are certain lawyers who specialise in stopping the presses at the last minute. However, if you can't afford to hire them, or they fail to stop the newspapers, then it's up to you to start your damage limitation.

One great technique is the all-out apology to family and friends. No one will question the fact that if they are your family and friends then surely you have their numbers and can call in person to apologise. There is no real need to apologise to them in the national press. Lets have a reality check: the apology isn't about them. It's about your career.

Remember, you're not really interested in them. This isn't about your personal life – you're saving your career and so all the apologising has to take place in the public arena.

Make sure you take all jokes on the chin and with good grace. Eventually all the mess will die down. The whole episode will help you develop a better 'heritage' and if you can survive this scandal in the long run it will work in your favour.

Modesty: the PR tool

Tip: When being interviewed about a film or production that's just won an award, you will find your natural instinct is to say,

Yes, I'm very hugely talented. Obviously I won the award because I'm great.

This kind of smugness doesn't go down well with the general public or with your colleagues. A way around this is to say things like:

Well, the whole thing was a team effort and it wouldn't have been possible without people like Joe Smith, who's an excellent casting director.

This is code for: He must be excellent to have cast me.

Jim Smith is an amazing director.

This is code for: Now filming is over I'm available for work and I'd like to be in his next production.

All the cast were brilliant. Jason Smith is a

tremendous actor, Jane Smith is a superb talent and it's a privilege to work opposite John Smith.

This is code for: And so by association I'm brilliant, I'm a tremendous actor, I'm a superb talent, because if I'm playing the lead in this production I'm at the very least as good as all these supporting actors who are all geniuses.

When using these codes it is acceptable to look very smug. In fact, usually it's unavoidable.

Once you've made a name for yourself you can either stay in acting or branch out into being a personality. The charity scam is a great way of keeping up your personal profile.

It is important to find a hook which will enable you to remain in the public eye in between jobs. A cause or a hobby will help you do this. If you bake cakes or are a keen fisherman, let everyone know.

Then you'll always make a good guest on a daytime TV show about cakes or fishing.

PR Essentials: Award shows and showbiz parties

Award shows are for the punters who prefer to be told what they like by entertainment experts. Very few people running showbiz really know what they like or want or what's really good or what indeed the punters like.

So award shows make all this easy. They just go for the bloke who's already got an award.

Many of these awards are decided by secret committees, which are often made up of agents and TV execs. who all have a vested interest in one act or another winning the award.

Winning an award doesn't mean you are the best. 'Best' is a meaningless concept in such a subjective area as art. (For the purposes of this paragraph I use 'art' to describe TV and films and acting.) The 'best' actor just might not have made a film that year.

You could have won the award because it was your turn, or your agent argued the toss on the committee, or you might be flavour of the month because of your recent work with charity or your wasting disease. Often people win awards because they are the biggest names available to collect an award on the night.

All an award can ever mean, even if judged fairly, is that a small band of people decided you were their favourite that year. Interpret this as you wish. But remember that this small band of people work in the industry and are not your target audience.

A lot of people secretly think award ceremonies are a load of baloney and often say so in acceptance speeches, dripping with sarcasm. But these same ungracious award winners also realise that awards will increase their earning power. And that's why they turn up to make those speeches instead of boycotting the award shows.

Exploiting Charities – Publicity with Other People's Money

Charity work can be a really great leg-up into the public consciousness at the start of your career, or to boost flagging popularity, or even just to give you the opportunity to move in a different direction.

If, for example, you are locked in a soap opera, boring yourself rigid but afraid to turn your back on the £80,000 a year to start life as a jobbing actress again, then a spot on a charity show could let you test the water. Your employers won't mind you experimenting on a show on another channel because it's 'for charity' and you will get the opportunity to be in a comedy sketch or show off your musical potential.

Just because it's a charity doesn't mean

you can't invoice for all your expenses. In most cases you can charge a charity a fee for your time and skills, although this won't be your usual fee. (Put your usual fee up and then 'discount' it for the charity.)

Choose the charity that suits your career. For example, if you are a footballer you might want to steer clear of landmine charities, in case they've missed one when you go for your photo shoot. There's not much a physiotherapist can do for you if you're missing your feet.

Charities are very happy for you to exploit them for the publicity as long as you pull in the money from the punters.

Obviously, it's unfair to suggest that all celebrities exploit charities for their own personal gain. The ones that don't are very difficult to spot but that's because they're discreetly making large donations to charities *away* from the glare of publicity.

Ghost columns

If you want to cash in by writing a celebrity column, but don't feel that you have any talent – don't worry. A lack of talent is no bar to journalistic greatness. The newspapers will happily supply you with a writer to 'help' mould your words.

Some celebrity magazine or newspaper contributors will make a token effort to write their own material – and will probably have it rewritten for them. Others stumble from bar to bar, mobile phone clutched to their ear, reporting in to the office on the other celebrities they're rubbing shoulders with, while newspaper editors and readers gleefully read their weekly bulletins from the front line, confident that they'll have the inside story on the inevitable and imminent meltdown when the heady lifestyle of drink and drug abuse gets too much.

Advertising and endorsements

Advertising is a great way to boost your income once you are famous. It's also a great way of becoming over-exposed.

Products to avoid:

★ Pills that induce weight loss.

★ Any products with adverts that are shot on video tape (rather than film and last longer than 30 seconds.

★ Anything that isn't available in the shops.

★ Any product featured in an advert where the phone number is repeated more than three times.

★ Nothing to do with bodily dysfunction.

★ No win no fee legal advice.

★ Anything that involves small ads in the back of the tabloids.

★ Old people's stuff, unless you're old.

Over-exposure can spell the end of your career and chasing the big bucks of endorsment and advertising is a very risky business. It's a fine line between being a familiar face and making a televisual nuisance of yourself. And those advertising executives who promised you an original and funny vehicle forgot to mention how irritating your quirky advert could become once it's on the telly a zillion times a day.

The public's resentment will multiply when they learn how many millions of pounds you've earned for telling them where to buy their groceries. And once they know how much money you earn, they'll realise you wouldn't be seen dead in the local supermarket. After all, you're far too rich. So not only have you become tedious to your audience, they also now feel patronised. Dangerous stuff.

So your career is in tatters. The adverts have alienated all your fans and you've run out of TV executives to bribe. What happens now?

Life After Fame

Fame is like an addictive drug and for many the come-down can be very hard – especially if you've blown all your money and ignored my advice about believing your own bullshit.

Most of us define ourselves by the job we do, so when we can no longer do our job we're going to feel very low. However, with fame there's the added problem that everyone else is all too aware you're no longer in the public eye. And they'll feel the need to inform you of that fact when they recognise you in the street.

If an emergency plumber stops being an emergency plumber he may feel a small sense of loss about not being able to charge a small fortune for replacing leaky washers or unblocking the toilet. But at least he doesn't get ribbed every time he goes out for not being an emergency plumber any more.

Life as a celebrity has-been can be very tough. But if that's how you end up, there's still hope for you. Remember that you were famous once and that you will always carry around a bit of residual fame, which can be easily exploited as long as you don't mind mucking in and getting your hands dirty.

There are plenty of jobs knocking around for the 'still a little bit famous'. For example, you could appear in one of those adverts that are only shown on digital TV, or you could present on one of the shopping channels. You could get a job as the communications officer for Rutland County Council, which may require you to give the occasional interview to the local news programmes.

If you're patient enough and if you have some genuine core skills you could come back into favour and your phone might start ringing once more.

It is worth offering a word of caution here: not all comebacks are genuine comebacks. Yours might be an ironic ruse by a TV producer or journalist who used to watch you on the telly when he was a kid, and who now has the power to give his own ego a boost by taking the piss out of you in front of an audience.

The best way to gauge whether your comeback is genuine or ironic is to consider how degrading the task is that you've been asked to perform. If the production team are being especially vague about details – even more than is usual for television – then alarm bells should start ringing. If you are required to swear or wear only your pants then the chances are that your comeback is definitely an ironic one.

On the plus side, the fee is the same for an ironic comeback as for a regular one and often an ironic comeback can lead to something more genuine. You should make the decision on whether or not to take part in an ironic comeback based on these four factors:

★ Your level of pride.

★ Your level of poverty.

★ How dull your life is with Rutland Council.

★ How degrading the task is you've been asked to perform.

Good luck.

A Final Thought

We've come to the end of our short journey together. It's time for me to depart and leave you to take your hesitant baby steps into the Hall of Fame alone.

Were you ever in the school play? Maybe you were Joseph or Mary, or a supporting character like the innkeeper or an oxen. If not, try and remember what it was like for the kids who were.

On the day after your first performance you were the centre of attention at school. Pupils and teachers gathered around you in the playground to tell you how good they thought you were. You can't have been *that* good – you were only six – but nevertheless you felt very special. You were well-known in your community. You were famous! One or two of the envious kids came along and teased you. They probably lured you out of the sight of the teachers so they could beat you up.

All this attention and criticism faded

once home time came and the holidays started, except when the bullies waited to finish you off by the school gates. And once you left school your fame vanished altogether and you returned to being just a regular kid again. You tried to do some showing off at home to get the kind of attention you had at school, but this only led to a thick ear and being sent to bed early. Your glory days were over.

You left school and got a job on the local radio station, broadcasting across the county. Everyone in your region knew who you were. A few sad anoraks would gather around you and ask you for signed photos. When you did a roadshow at the county fair you attracted quite a crowd. A few envious blokes would shout abuse at you from the beer tent. But still, when you went away for the weekend to the next county nobody knew who you were.

Then you landed a job on a national TV station, or maybe it was a sports show in the middle of the night. You were the darling of insomniac sport fans everywhere. When you went to a football match or a late-night kebab shop people slapped you on your back and offered you a bite of their kebab. The envious still spat in your chilli sauce while you weren't looking. But you lost your fame the minute you went to a nice middle-class dinner party with people who had proper jobs and didn't stay up late to watch sports shows.

The same thing happened when you landed a mainstream national TV show. People would stop you in the street to say they loved the show and the envious would write bitter things about you in the press. You'd be the centre of attention until you left the country to go abroad and there you'd no longer be famous.

Even if you became the most famous person on the planet you'd still have to consider that Earth is smaller than a speck of dust compared with the size of infinite space and as space is infinite there is an infinite chance that there are an infinite number of planets just like Earth and there is an infinite probability that these planets are populated with an infinite number of people just like us. None of whom will ever have ever seen your work and none of whom will know who you are. That's a hell of a lot of people who have never heard of you.

Another Final Note

Unfortunately there are many cynics who attack fame and those who wannabe famous. They liken the desire to be famous to a disease and they think that those who have that desire are in some way mentally ill. They say that if fame only exists in the mind of those around you, then it's not real and you shouldn't waste your life trying to achieve it.

They say any immortality that you might achieve through being famous will vanish once everyone who's heard of you is dead.

The cynics who think they have good advice to offer will say that, given the state of the world today, you are much better off keeping your head down and maintaining a low profile. They say, save yourself a lifetime of heartache, low self-esteem and disappointment and take up a pursuit that is worthwhile, one that will have long-term benefits for all of mankind, as this is the only way that you will find genuine happiness.

I know that these sound like the words of a crazed escapee from a lunatic asylum but these cynics are out there and these views do exist. It takes all sorts.